Middle Level Programs and Practices In Elementary Schools:

Report of a National Study

C. Kenneth McEwin
William M. Alexander

NATIONAL MIDDLE SCHOOL ASSOCIATION

nmsa

Drs. C. Kenneth McEwin and William M. Alexander have combined their talents on a number of important professional projects. The middle school movement and the National Middle School Association are indebted to them for their research studies, the most recent of which is presented in this monograph.

Dr. McEwin, Professor and Chairperson of Curriculum and Instruction at Appalachian State University, Boone, North Carolina is a former NMSA president. Dr. Alexander, Professor Emeritus of Education at the University of Florida, Gainesville was the earliest advocate of the middle school.

Appreciation is also expressed to Hilda Moretz, secretary to Dr. McEwin, to Media Services, Appalachian State University, and to Mary Mitchell, assistant to the editor.

Copyright © 1990 by the National Middle School Association
4807 Evanswood Drive, Columbus, Ohio 43229
$6.00

The materials presented herein are the expressions of the author and do not necessarily represent the policies of NMSA.

Printed in the United States of America by
Panaprint, Inc., P. O. Box 10297, Macon, GA 31297

ISBN: 1-56090-050-4

Table of Contents

List of Tables

Foreword

Early adolescence is a stage of life. Youngsters from approximately ten to fourteen years old comprise this period between childhood and full adolescence. It is developmentally determined and is only indirectly related to school organization. So an eleven or twelve year old that is housed in an elementary school is just as much an early adolescent as one who is housed in a middle school. Developmentally and educationally the needs of both are the same. Those moving into and through puberty ought to have exploratory activities, a comprehensive health and physical education program, and socialization experiences, to give three examples. Whether such needs can be effectively met in an elementary school is a fair question. On the other hand, intermediate schools are often so large and so impersonal that they have trouble adequately meeting the continuing need of these still immature youths for security in personal relationships. So no either-or situation exists.

The interest generated by the middle school movement has been primarily focussed on organizing and dealing with 6-8 schools or reorganizing 7-9 schools to become 6-8 schools. The thousands and thousands of early adolescents who have continued to receive their education in the older traditional K-8 elementary schools have been, therefore, largely ignored.

The study reported here, then, is especially pertinent. It is the first comprehensive study that specifically assesses "middle school practices" in grades 6, 7, and 8 when those grades are part of an elementary school. It further makes comparisons between the status of those practices in elementary schools and their status in middle and junior high schools. The findings are essential baseline data. As Abraham Lincoln observed, "If we could first know where we are, and whither we are tending, we could better judge what to do, and how to do it."

Thanks to the cooperative efforts of these two experienced educators we now know the general nature of these middle grades when they are housed in elementary schools relative to commonly recognized characteristics of middle level schools. Thus armed we can better judge what changes are needed to make such situations developmentally more appropriate.

John H. Lounsbury
Editor, NMSA Publications

I

Introduction

Recently conducted studies of separately organized middle level schools have provided a rather complete description of their programs and practices (Cawelti, 1988; Alexander & McEwin, 1989b). Less is known, however, about programs and practices in those middle grades (6 through 8) when they are located in elementary schools. Many thousands of young adolescents attend these 5,552 K/1-8 elementary schools including approximately nine percent of all seventh graders (National Center for Educational Statistics, 1989; Epstein & Mac Iver, 1990).

The reordering of American education to consist of three levels — elementary, middle, and high school — has raised many questions about the practice of housing both elementary and middle grades in the same school. Paramount among these are: "What is the nature of middle grades programs and practices in combination elementary-middle schools?" " How do the programs and practices in these schools compare with those of separately organized middle and junior high schools?" "Should the middle grades be in an elementary school?"

The authors of this report previously conducted a survey of separately organized middle grades schools to determine what changes had occurred in these middle level schools in a twenty year period and to determine likenesses and differences which existed between the various grade organization patterns of these schools. This survey was primarily a replication of one conducted by Alexander in 1967-68. The data of the 1987-88 survey, including relevant data from the 1967-68 one, are reported elsewhere (Alexander & McEwin, 1989a; Alexander & McEwin, 1989b). To complete the comparison of various grade organizations the additional survey reported here was conducted in 1988-89 of schools that contained grades K or 1-8.

A national random sample of 300 schools was selected. Of these, 152 (51 percent) returned the completed survey forms, with 145 (95 percent) of those being K-8 and 7 (5 percent) being grades 1-8. The presence or absence of a kindergarten was not considered significant to this study and therefore the data for K-8 and 1-8 schools are not separated and these schools are often indicated simply as K-8 in the remainder of this report.

The 1988-89 survey form (see Appendix) was essentially the same as that used for the 1987-88 survey, although necessary changes were made for the questions to be fully applicable to the K-8 plan and its comparison with the

1

other organizational plans for the middle grades. In the present report, major attention is given to comparing three organizational types for the grades usually considered as middle grades: (1) elementary school types (grades 5-8 or 6-8 in K/1-8 schools); (2) middle school types (grades 5-8, 6-8); (3) junior high school types (grades 7-8, 7-9).

Most middle school and all junior high school types included in our surveys do not include grade 5, junior high types do not include grade 6, and grade 9 is included only in grades 7-9 junior highs. Only grades 7 and 8 are common to all these grade organizations. Furthermore, the two grade organizations in the middle and junior high groups are generally much alike. Therefore most of the data in this report are for these grade organizations: grades 6-8 in elementary schools; grades 6-8 middle schools; and grades 7-9 junior high schools. Thus the comparisons can be and are for grade 6 only in the elementary and middle school types, and for grades 7-8 in all three types.

A concluding section presents a partial appraisal of the practice of including middle grades in the K-8 organization. Primary reference is made to the same criteria of separate programs for the middle schools as were used in our earlier survey reports. It should be noted, too, that these six criteria, although stated somewhat differently, are encompassed in the recommendations presented in *Turning Points: Preparing American Youth for the 21st Century* (1989), the strong argument of the Carnegie Task Force on Education of Young Adolescents for improving the education and life of young adolescents, ages 10-15. The Carnegie report makes emphatic the point that: "Middle grade schools — junior high, intermediate, and middle schools — are potentially society's most powerful force to recapture millions of youth adrift, and help every young person thrive during early adolescence" (p. 8). The document then presents in detail eight recommendations for transforming middle grade schools so that they can achieve their potential. We believe that our six criteria correspond to these with the exception of the Carnegie ones dealing with families and communities. Although we heartily endorse these recommendations we consider them beyond the scope of our studies.

II

Characteristics of Grades 6-8 in Elementary Schools As Compared With Middle And Junior High Schools

As indicated in the introductory section the characteristics of middle school grades programs included in this survey are those originally identified for Alexander's 1968 survey of reorganized middle schools, plus a few additions from our 1988 one. No effort was made to identify characteristics that would be unique to the elementary type organization. Each of the following sections reports the data for at least one organization, usually two, in addition to the elementary one (any comparisons for grade 6 exclude the grades 7-9 junior high).

Enrollment
Smallness tends to be characteristic of the elementary type of organization. As shown in Table 1, the modal percent (22) in the elementary type (K-8) of organization is in the 1-100 enrollment category, but in the middle school type it is 501-600, and in the junior high, 701-800. In the elementary type, 81 percent had enrollments less than 501, as compared with those in middle and junior high types of 42 and 29 percent, respectively. Only 1 percent of the elementary type have over 1000 students, as compared with 8 percent of the middle, and 15 percent of the junior high types. Furthermore, it should be noted that the enrollments given are for the entire school, that is for just 3 grades in the middle and junior high school types as compared with 8 (plus kindergarten in 95 percent) of the elementary type. Clearly the opportunity for more flexible and closer interpersonal relationships is available in the elementary type. Thus, on the size factor the K-8 grade organization meets well the Carnegie Task Force recommendation of smaller size learning communities for the middle grades. It does not follow, as shown later in this report, that the teaming and teacher advisory programs also recommended are widely used in these schools. Also, one should be wary of the tendency to assume that small schools are necessarily better schools. Many other complex factors that influence schooling practices should also be considered.

Housing Arrangements
As shown in Table 2, over two-thirds of the elementary type schools house the middle grades in the same plant as all other grades (K/1-5), whereas 80 and 82 percent of the middle and junior high types respectively had their three grades in separate buildings. Especially desirable in the larger schools, the school-within-a-school plan long recommended by educational authorities and strongly reiterated by the Carnegie Task Force has been adopted in few schools of the types currently under consideration. Having any of the middle grades scattered in separate buildings is undesirable, but it is uncertain whether those checking this

3

report for the elementary type meant any of grades 6-8 or of all grades. A major weakness of many elementary type middle grades plans is the housing of children ranging from 5 to 15 years of age in the same building. Especially in crowded ones, both the younger and older groups are often disadvantaged.

TABLE 1
PERCENTS OF SCHOOLS BY DIFFERENT
GRADE ORGANIZATIONS HAVING CERTAIN
ENROLLMENTS

Range of Enrollments	Percent of Schools in Surveys		
	Elementary K/1-8	Middle Gr. 6-8	Jr. High Gr. 7-9
1 - 100	22	<1	<1
101 - 200	14	4	2
201 - 300	17	12	8
301 - 400	15	11	8
401 - 500	13	14	10
501 - 600	5	19	8
601 - 700	5	13	12
701 - 800	4	10	19
801 - 900	2	5	12
901 - 1000	2	3	6
1001 - 1100	0	3	8
1101 - 1200	0	2	5
1201 - 1300	1	2	1
Above 1300	0	1	1

TABLE 2
PERCENTS OF SCHOOLS BY DIFFERENT GRADE ORGANIZATIONS HAVING HAVING VARIOUS TYPES OF HOUSING ARRANGEMENTS

Housing Arrangements	Percent of Schools in Surveys		
	Elementary K/1-8	Middle Gr. 6-8	Jr. High Gr. 7-9
One Plant (all grades)	68	80	82
School Within a School Each a Separate Area	5	6	4
Certain Grades in Separate Buildings on Same Campus	19	7	5
Some Students Housed On Another Campus	2	3	4

Dates of Establishment

As the newcomer in American school organization, it was to be expected that middle schools would have been established most recently, and Table 3 shows that 95 percent have been established since 1962. Similarly, over three-quarters of the traditional eight-grade elementary schools had been established before 1955. The abrupt drop in establishing new junior high schools came in the 1980's, only 4 percent being established in this decade.

TABLE 3
PERCENTS OF SCHOOLS BY DIFFERENT GRADE ORGANIZATIONS HAVING CERTAIN DATES OF ESTABLISHMENT

Years	Percent of Schools in Surveys		
	Elementary K/1-8	Middle Gr. 6-8	Jr. High Gr. 7-9
Before 1955	77	2	20
1956 - 1962	6	3	22
1963 - 1971	9	25	29
1972 - 1979	7	35	25
1980 - 1987	2	35	4

Measures of Articulation

The percents of schools using certain means of articulation did not vary greatly. However, it can be noted from Table 4 that somewhat smaller percents of elementary organizations reported use of "joint workshops with teachers in

5

lower and higher grades," "joint curriculum planning of activities with teachers of higher and/or lower grades," and "middle school students taking advanced course work in the high school."

TABLE 4
PERCENTS OF SCHOOLS BY DIFFERENT GRADES USING CERTAIN MEANS OF ARTICULATION

Means of Articulation	Percent of Schools in Surveys		
	Elementary K/1-8	Middle Gr. 6-8	Jr. High Gr. 7-9
Joint Workshops With Teachers in Lower and Higher Grades	56	70	71
Joint Curriculum Planning Activities With Teachers of Higher and/or Lower Grades	49	66	68
Obtaining or Providing Data *re* Students Entering or Leaving Your School	73	78	88
Student Visitation of High School(s) for Orientation	74	73	61
Visitation of Your School by High School Representatives for the purpose of Orientation	68	72	70
Middle School Students Taking Advanced Course Work in the High School	16	31	37

Subjects Taken by All Students Each Grade

Table 5 shows that the basic subjects of language arts, math, science, social studies, and physical education are even more universally required of all students in each middle grade in the elementary than the other types. These basics are 100 percent required in the elementary type, with a slight decline in the middle and junior high in social studies and science, and a more marked one in physical education. The pressure of popular elective alternatives, such as music, is undoubtedly responsible for the decrease in physical education in middle and junior high schools.

Traditional Exploratory Subjects

A frequent argument for putting grades 6-8 in a separate school has been that of having in the newer plant those facilities necessary for exploratory courses. Table 6 shows support for this argument so far as required home economics and industrial arts in grade 6 are concerned. A larger percent of elementary type middle grades offers required music, with a larger percent of middle schools offering it as elective, and the situation is similar in art also for grade 6. In

6

TABLE 5
**PERCENTS OF SCHOOLS BY DIFFERENT GRADE
ORGANIZATIONS REPORTING CERTAIN SUBJECTS
TAKEN ALL YEAR EACH GRADE BY ALL STUDENTS**

Subjects	Percent of Schools in Surveys		
	Elementary K/1-8	Middle Gr. 6-8	Jr. High Gr. 7-9
Language Arts	100	99	99
Mathematics	100	100	100
Social Studies	100	96	89
Science	100	94	81
Physical Education	97	80	70

grades 7 and 8 (see Tables 7 and 8) the percents of elementary schools requiring art, music and reading are larger, with a corresponding increase of middle and junior high schools offering these exploratory courses as elective. Home economics and industrial arts are now widely available, both as required and elective courses in grades 7 and 8 in middle and junior high schools. Foreign language as an elective is also more widely available in these latter grades and types. Thus the chances of a middle grades student having these various traditional exploratory courses does seem somewhat better in the separate middle level schools, but still possible in many of the elementary type ones.

Certain Newer Exploratory Subjects
Tables 9, 10 and 11 show clearly the strong relationship between current developments in our society and the introduction and requirements of related courses in schools. Thus instruction in Computers, Health, and Sex Education has become very common in the middle grades, reflecting the national trend toward computer usage and the national concern for the healthy development of young adolescents. A Careers course, too, has been introduced in these grades, and Creative Writing has become more common. Each of these courses is more frequently required than elective at all three grade levels in each type of school. Only in grade 8 of junior highs is Journalism offered by as much as 20 percent of the schools, and Agriculture has never caught on in the middle grades.

So far as comparisons by grade organization are concerned, the elementary type does not seem to be behind the others in offering the popular newer courses. In all three grades it has a larger percent of required courses in Computers, Creative Writing, Health and Sex Education than the other types with only small differences as to elective ones. In both surveys numerous other courses were added by individual schools; for example, in the elementary survey those write-ins of required subjects included "Navajo Studies," "Study Skills," "Drama," and "Library," and as elective, "Guitars," "Karate," "CPR/Life Saving," and "Office Aide."

TABLE 6
PERCENTS OF SCHOOLS BY DIFFERENT GRADE ORGANIZATIONS OFFERING CERTAIN TRADITIONAL EXPLORATORY COURSES AS REQUIRED AND ELECTIVE SUBJECTS, GRADE 6

Subjects	Percent of Schools in Surveys	
	Elementary K/1-8	Middle Gr. 6-8
Art		
Required	77	63
Elective	10	22
Foreign Language		
Required	7	8
Elective	3	12
Home Economics		
Required	5	34
Elective	3	10
Industrial Arts		
Required	7	36
Elective	3	10
Music		
Required	66	49
Elective	6	17
Reading		
Required	90	85
Elective	1	1

TABLE 7
**PERCENTS OF SCHOOLS BY DIFFERENT
GRADE ORGANIZATIONS OFFERING CERTAIN
TRADITIONAL EXPLORATORY COURSES
AS REQUIRED AND ELECTIVE SUBJECTS, GRADE 7**

Subjects	Percent of Schools in Surveys		
	Elementary K/1-8	Middle Gr. 6-8	Jr. High Gr. 7-9
Art			
Required	71	46	43
Elective	18	41	41
Foreign Language			
Required	7	10	11
Elective	6	29	32
Home Economics			
Required	5	36	26
Elective	9	33	28
Industrial Arts			
Required	18	38	29
Elective	7	32	27
Music			
Required	59	31	35
Elective	6	20	27
Reading			
Required	83	70	50
Elective	1	5	21

9

TABLE 8
PERCENTS OF SCHOOLS BY DIFFERENT
GRADE ORGANIZATIONS OFFERING CERTAIN
TRADITIONAL EXPLORATORY COURSES
AS REQUIRED AND ELECTIVE SUBJECTS, GRADE 8

Subjects	Percent of Schools in Surveys		
	Elementary K/1-8	Middle Gr. 6-8	Jr. High Gr. 7-9
Art			
Required	69	34	31
Elective	18	52	56
Foreign Language			
Required	13	8	11
Elective	7	42	50
Home Economics			
Required	21	30	26
Elective	11	47	43
Industrial Arts			
Required	20	29	30
Elective	9	47	45
Music			
Required	57	21	23
Elective	7	21	24
Reading			
Required	82	58	33
Elective	1	54	29

TABLE 9
PERCENTS OF SCHOOLS BY DIFFERENT
GRADE ORGANIZATIONS OFFERING
CERTAIN NEWER EXPLORATORY
COURSES AS REQUIRED AND
ELECTIVE SUBJECTS, GRADE 6

Subjects	Percent of Schools in Surveys	
	Elementary K/1-8	Middle Gr. 6-8
Agriculture Required	0	1
Elective	0	0
Careers Required	9	6
Elective	0	4
Computers Required	45	38
Elective	12	11
Creative Writing Required	41	23
Elective	3	3
Health Required	73	59
Elective	1	1
Journalism Required	2	1
Elective	3	3
Sex Education Required	30	23
Elective	3	3

TABLE 10
PERCENTS OF SCHOOLS BY DIFFERENT
GRADE ORGANIZATIONS OFFERING CERTAIN NEWER
EXPLORATORY COURSES AS REQUIRED AND
ELECTIVE SUBJECTS, GRADE 7

Subjects	Percent of Schools in Surveys		
	Elementary K/1-8	Middle Gr. 6-8	Jr. High Gr. 7-9
Agriculture			
Required	0	1	<1
Elective	0	0	1
Careers			
Required	16	9	9
Elective	1	7	8
Computers			
Required	53	40	20
Elective	13	19	21
Creative Writing			
Required	43	23	13
Elective	3	5	8
Health			
Required	70	58	57
Elective	1	3	3
Journalism			
Required	4	1	0
Elective	5	11	8
Sex Education			
Required	32	27	16
Elective	5	5	2

TABLE 11

PERCENTS OF SCHOOLS BY DIFFERENT GRADE ORGANIZATIONS OFFERING CERTAIN NEWER EXPLORATORY COURSES AS REQUIRED AND ELECTIVE SUBJECTS, GRADE 8

Subjects	Percent of Schools in Surveys		
	Elementary K/1-8	Middle Gr. 6-8	Jr. High Gr. 7-9
Agriculture Required	81	1	2
Elective	0	2	4
Careers Required	20	12	12
Elective	1	10	12
Computers Required	55	37	24
Elective	15	25	26
Creative Writing Required	43	24	14
Elective	3	6	7
Health Required	72	57	52
Elective	1	3	2
Journalism Required	4	1	0
Elective	6	19	20
Sex Education Required	53	26	13
Elective	5	5	4

Other Curriculum Opportunities

Tables 12, 13, and 14 show the relative percents of schools offering various additional clubs and activities in grades 6, 7, and 8, respectively.

In grade 6, boys and girls in the middle school type are more likely than those in the elementary one to participate in Intramural Sports and less likely to be involved in Interschool Sports. In grades 7 and 8, the same situation prevails as to Intramural Sports in both middle and junior high types as compared with the elementary, but the percents of middle schools and junior highs having Interschool Sports in grades 7 and 8 are slightly higher than those of the elementary type. Educators and others who believe in the superiority of intramural over interscholastic athletic activities for growing children ages 10-14 will be concerned about the general availability of interscholastics, and look towards reduction in these and an increase in intramurals.

As to the other opportunities listed in Tables 12-14, only Arts and Crafts was about as widely available in all three types in all grades. The others tended to be more frequently available in the middle and junior high types, with Honor Society in grade 8 being in an appreciably smaller percent of the elementary type. Photography, Publications, School Parties, Social Dancing, and Student

TABLE 12
PERCENTS OF SCHOOLS BY DIFFERENT GRADE ORGANIZATIONS OFFERING CERTAIN OTHER CURRICULUM OPPORTUNITIES, GRADE 6

Activity	Percent of Schools in Surveys	
	Elementary K/1-8	Middle Gr. 6-8
Arts and Crafts	34	38
Honor Society	26	39
Intramural Sports (Boys)	41	69
Intramural Sports (Girls)	41	68
Interschool Sports (Boys)	50	30
Interschool Sports (Girls)	49	30
Photography	0	11
Publications	9	38
School Parties	50	56
Social Dancing	30	55
Student Council	34	83

Council were checked as available by smaller percents of elementary than middle and junior high types for all grades, with the difference greatest for Student Council (approximately half of the other).

Again, many other activities were listed by individual schools in response to the write-in ("others") space in both surveys. Interesting examples listed in the elementary school survey included: "Academic Super Bowl," "Chess," "Quiz Bowl," "Public Speaking," and "Peer Leadership."

TABLE 13
PERCENTS OF SCHOOLS BY DIFFERENT GRADE
ORGANIZATIONS OFFERING CERTAIN OTHER
CURRICULUM OPPORTUNITIES, GRADE 7

Activity	Percent of Schools in Surveys		
	Elementary K/1-8	Middle Gr. 6-8	Jr. High Gr. 7-9
Arts and Crafts	34	38	42
Honor Society	26	39	32
Intramural Sports (Boys)	45	69	59
Intramural Sports (Girls)	45	68	60
Interschool Sports (Boys)	67	72	79
Interschool Sports (Girls)	65	72	80
Photography	1	15	16
Publications	23	50	45
School Parties	53	55	58
Social Dancing	49	66	67
Student Council	44	86	93

TABLE 14
PERCENTS OF SCHOOLS BY DIFFERENT GRADE
ORGANIZATIONS OFFERING CERTAIN OTHER
CURRICULUM OPPORTUNITIES, GRADE 8

Activity	Percent of Schools in Surveys		
	Elementary K/1-8	Middle Gr. 6-8	Jr. High Gr. 7-9
Arts and Crafts	35	39	41
Honor Society	26	41	51
Intramural Sports (Boys)	45	66	57
Intramural Sports (Girls)	45	66	58
Interschool Sports (Boys)	67	77	83
Interschool Sports (Girls)	65	75	84
Photography	1	21	21
Publications	27	62	58
School Parties	53	57	58
Social Dancing	50	69	67
Student Council	45	89	93

Instructional Organization Plans

Data regarding the instructional organization used in teaching the four basic subjects in each grade in the types of schools being compared are presented in Tables 15, 16 and 17. The following comparative results may be noted:

1.   Somewhat surprisingly, in view of the traditional self-contained classroom organization of the elementary school, the percent of elementary schools having departmentalization in grade 6, 7, and 8 is almost as large as in the middle school type. However, the percent of elementary school types having the interdisciplinary team plan in grade 6 is less than half that of the middle school types while the percent having the self-contained classroom plan is more than twice that of the middle school types.

2.   The elementary type has a still larger (approximately 3 times greater for departmentalized as for self-contained) percent of schools having departmentalization in grade 7, and only about 10 percent with the interdisciplinary team plan. The percents of middle and junior high schools having the interdisciplinary team and the self-contained classroom plans in grades 7 and 8 are lower than those of the middle school type in grade 6, with departmentalization especially leading in grade 8 (87 percent in the junior high types in all subjects). It should be noted, however, that some schools checked

16

more than one plan per subject because of the use of more than one organizational plan, and therefore some columns add to more than 100 percent. In a few schools, usually the larger ones, more than one organizational plan was used even at the same grade level.

3. The greatest use of interdisciplinary team organization is in the middle school type (from about 25 percent in grade 8 to over 30 percent in grade 7, and almost 40 percent in grade 6). The greatest use of departmentalization is in the junior high school type, where it is used in about two-thirds of all the schools in grade 7 and 8, and even more in grade 8 of junior high types, as noted above. The use of the self-contained classroom plan is highest in the elementary type, all subjects and grades, and lowest in the junior high school type, all subjects, grades 7-8 (no grade 6 in this type).

4. Some very interesting notes from elementary school respondents in the "Others" space for the question on instructional organization emphasize the extremely small size of many of these schools. For example, two schools were one-room schools, housing all pupils, all grades, in the single classroom. Another was a two-teacher school, these teachers handling all subjects except music (itinerant teacher), and another had one teacher with the following enrollments at the grade levels indicated: K-1, one; grades 2-4, one; grades 5-8, one. This school did have part-time physical education and music teachers. Still another school reported "we do some work with students across grade levels (multi-age)." Flexibility in scheduling and in subject/grade plans would seem relatively easy in such situations, but four-teacher teaming is obviously out.

TABLE 15
PERCENTS OF SCHOOLS BY DIFFERENT
GRADE ORGANIZATIONS USING
CERTAIN PLANS* FOR ORGANIZING
INSTRUCTION IN BASIC SUBJECTS,
GRADE 6

| Subjects | Percent of Schools in Surveys | | | | | |
| | Elementary K/1-8 | | | Middle Gr. 6-8 | | |
	IT	D	SC	IT	D	SC
Language Arts	14	41	41	41	46	18
Mathematics	13	41	41	38	50	14
Science	11	41	41	37	50	14
Social Studies	11	43	41	39	47	15

*IT = Interdisciplinary Team
D = Departmentalization
SC = Self-Contained Classroom

TABLE 16
**PERCENTS OF SCHOOLS BY DIFFERENT
GRADE ORGANIZATIONS USING CERTAIN
PLANS* FOR ORGANIZING INSTRUCTION IN
BASIC SUBJECTS, GRADE 7**

| Subjects | Percent of Schools in Surveys | | | | | | | | |
| | Elementary K/1-8 | | | Middle Gr. 6-8 | | | Jr. High Gr. 7-9 | | |
	IT	D	SC	IT	D	SC	IT	D	SC
Language Arts	10	66	22	35	60	7	18	83	9
Mathematics	9	66	22	30	67	6	11	84	9
Science	9	67	22	29	67	5	11	84	9
Social Studies	13	67	22	32	63	5	15	83	9

*IT = Interdisciplinary Team
 D = Departmentalization
SC = Self-Contained Classroom

TABLE 17
**PERCENTS OF SCHOOLS BY DIFFERENT
GRADE ORGANIZATIONS USING CERTAIN
PLANS* FOR ORGANIZING INSTRUCTION IN
BASIC SUBJECTS, GRADE 8**

| Subjects | Percent of Schools in Surveys | | | | | | | | |
| | Elementary K/1-8 | | | Middle Gr. 6-8 | | | Jr. High Gr. 7-9 | | |
	IT	D	SC	IT	D	SC	IT	D	SC
Language Arts	9	66	23	29	67	6	14	87	9
Mathematics	9	66	23	25	72	5	9	87	9
Science	8	67	23	24	72	5	9	87	9
Social Studies	12	67	23	26	68	5	11	87	9

*IT = Interdisciplinary Team
 D = Departmentalization
SC = Self-Contained Classroom

Criteria for Grouping Students

Tables 18, 19, and 20 show the percents of schools of the three grade organizations using certain criteria for grouping students, by grades, for the purposes of basic subjects, elective subjects, and advisory programs. These comparisons are noted:

1. Intelligence quotients are used less frequently in grouping for basic subjects at all three grades in the elementary type, and in fact less frequently than other criteria in each type of school at all three grades.
2. Achievement tests are used in larger percents of the elementary type for grouping in elective subjects and advisory programs, and smaller percents in basic subjects, than the middle and junior high types.
3. Teacher recommendations were used in about equal percents of elementary and middle school types, all grades in basic subjects, but by larger percents of the former in elective subjects and advisory programs.
4. Age (number of years in school) was used by larger percents of the elementary than other types in all grades included for each purpose, although the differences were smaller for grouping in basic subjects.
5. Previous academic record was used by about two-thirds of each type and in each grade for basic subjects, with considerably less use for electives and advisory groups (though more in elementary and junior high) for the latter.
6. Random assignment (no criterion for grouping) was used in about one-fourth of all types and grades for basic subjects; for over half of the elementary and middle types and slightly less in junior high for elective subjects; and in over 40 percent of elementary and junior high, all grades, slightly less in middle school, for advisory programs.

In general, it is clear that no one criterion is used for grouping for any purpose. The arbitrary use of IQ and achievement test records only is not indicated. The use of teachers' own judgments seems extensive, with this criterion getting the highest percent of any type, all grades, for basic subjects and elective subjects and highest in the elementary type for advisory programs. The elementary type seems the most willing to use the least selective criteria — random assignment, age, teacher recommendations — although achievement tests and previous academic record also were used by large percents of this type.

Scheduling of Instruction

Table 21 shows that the once typical self-contained classroom schedule (that is, a more or less flexible schedule controlled by the classroom teacher and presumably unique to each class) of the elementary school is no longer dominant at least in the middle grades. The uniform daily period prevails in over half (53 percent) of the schools in grade 6, and over two-thirds in grades 7 and 8. This schedule, once characteristic of only the high school, is provided in even larger percents at all grades of middle and junior high schools. Flexible scheduling was indicated for small percents of the elementary schools, and larger ones by about a quarter of the middle schools and less than 10 percent in grades 7 and 8 of junior high schools.

19

TABLE 18
**PERCENTS OF SCHOOLS BY DIFFERENT GRADE
ORGANIZATIONS GROUPING STUDENTS IN BASIC SUBJECTS
ACCORDING TO CERTAIN CRITERIA, IN GRADES 6, 7 AND 8**

Type of Scheduling	Grade	Percent of Schools in Surveys		
		Elementary K/1-8	Middle Gr. 6-8	Jr. High Gr. 7-9
Intelligence Quotient	6	10	27	-
	7	11	28	31
	8	12	27	31
Achievement Tests	6	52	68	-
	7	57	70	72
	8	58	68	72
Teacher Recommendations	6	71	76	-
	7	72	79	77
	8	73	78	77
Age (Number of Years in School)	6	28	22	-
	7	29	21	17
	8	28	22	17
Previous Academic Record	6	61	61	-
	7	63	65	69
	8	63	64	69
Random Assignment	6	26	25	-
	7	28	24	26
	8	28	25	26

20

TABLE 19
**PERCENTS OF SCHOOLS BY DIFFERENT GRADE
ORGANIZATIONS GROUPING STUDENTS IN ELECTIVE SUBJECTS
ACCORDING TO CERTAIN CRITERIA, IN GRADES 6, 7 AND 8**

Type of Scheduling	Grade	Percent of Schools in Surveys		
		Elementary K/1-8	Middle Gr. 6-8	Jr. High Gr. 7-9
Intelligence Quotient	6	10	3	-
	7	12	4	10
	8	12	4	10
Achievement Tests	6	26	8	-
	7	28	9	20
	8	28	10	21
Teacher Recommendations	6	48	21	-
	7	48	22	31
	8	48	25	34
Age (Number of Years in School)	6	19	8	-
	7	16	8	8
	8	16	8	8
Previous Academic Record	6	17	12	-
	7	20	13	33
	8	20	14	34
Random Assignment	6	57	50	-
	7	56	54	42
	8	56	54	44

TABLE 20
**PERCENTS OF SCHOOLS BY DIFFERENT GRADE ORGANIZATIONS
GROUPING STUDENTS IN ADVISORY PROGRAMS ACCORDING
TO CERTAIN CRITERIA, IN GRADES 6, 7 AND 8**

Type of Scheduling	Grade	Percent of Schools in Surveys		
		Elementary K/1-8	Middle Gr. 6-8	Jr. High Gr. 7-9
Intelligence Quotient	6	6	5	-
	7	7	5	10
	8	6	4	10
Achievement Tests	6	35	13	-
	7	33	11	20
	8	33	11	21
Teacher Recommendations	6	48	16	-
	7	47	14	31
	8	47	14	34
Age (Number of Years in School)	6	30	11	-
	7	29	10	8
	8	29	10	8
Previous Academic Record	6	36	10	-
	7	34	10	30
	8	33	9	34
Random Assignment	6	43	34	-
	7	43	35	42
	8	43	35	44

TABLE 21
PERCENTS OF SCHOOLS BY DIFFERENT GRADE
ORGANIZATIONS USING CERTAIN TYPES OF
SCHEDULING FOR INSTRUCTION, BY GRADE

Type of Scheduling	Grade	Percent of Schools in Surveys		
		Elementary K/1-8	Middle Gr. 6-8	Jr. High Gr. 7-9
Self-Contained Classroom	6	45	20	-
	7	25	9	16
	8	25	9	16
Daily Periods— Uniform Length	6	53	74	-
	7	68	83	93
	8	68	85	95
Flexible Scheduling	6	9	30	-
	7	4	25	8
	8	4	21	7
Daily Periods— Varying Length	6	16	12	-
	7	16	11	2
	8	16	10	2

The relative smallness of the elementary type of middle grade organization would seem to facilitate more informal types of instructional arrangements and schedules. The adoption of high school departmentalization and uniform daily periods was probably natural in earlier decades of this century as the upper elementary grades were brought under the control of the secondary schools. Later, with the advent of middle schools, the elementary ones may now need to take a new look at those practices.

Independent Study Opportunities
Table 22 shows the elementary type scores well on the provision of independent study opportunities. On the first listed opportunity, release from class part or all of the time for such study, 60 percent or more of the elementary type at each grade provide such arrangements as compared with 25 percent or slightly more in the middle school and junior high types. Also over 40 percent of the elementary schools as compared with about 20 percent of the middle schools and slightly less in the junior highs have individually planned programs with regularly scheduled independent study times. As to the other opportunities, seminars and work experiences, there is little difference between the three organizations.

TABLE 22
PERCENTS OF SCHOOLS BY DIFFERENT GRADE ORGANIZATIONS PROVIDING CERTAIN TYPES OF INDEPENDENT STUDY OPPORTUNITIES, BY GRADE

| Study Opportunity | Grade | Percent of Schools in Surveys | | |
		Elementary K/1-8	Middle Gr. 6-8	Jr. High Gr. 7-9
Some students are released part or all of the time from the class(es) for independent study	6	60	25	-
	7	64	27	27
	8	66	26	29
One or more groups of students with similar interests work as a seminair	6	22	12	-
	7	19	14	13
	8	20	14	14
Some students have individually-planned programs with regularly scheduled time for independent study	6	43	18	-
	7	44	20	17
	8	46	22	16
Some students have time scheduled for work experience with faculty supervision	6	8	7	-
	7	14	8	11
	8	15	11	12

Reports of Student Progress

Table 23 shows that relatively small differences exist between the three types of grade organization as to the type of student progress reports used. The word scale (Excellent, Good, Fair, etc.) is used in 31 percent of the elementary as compared with 21 and 11 percent of the middle and junior high school types respectively. Unsatisfactory/Satisfactory marks are used in 55 percent of the elementary as compared with 39 and 27 percent in the middle and junior high types, respectively. Regular parent/teacher conferences are held in 89 percent of elementary as compared with 67 and 55 percent of the middle and junior high types.

Thus, the elementary organization tends to utilize non-letter scale marks somewhat more frequently than the others, although the Satisfactory/Unsatisfactory scale is an arbitrary one certainly needing supplementary information that could come in conference situations. Several of the survey respondents used the open-ended space ("other") to report specific plans of supplementary reporting, including "two parent nights each school year," "regular scheduled interim reports," "progress report each 9 weeks," "weekly grades for students with academic problems," "contact with parent by

24

teacher when needed," "3 and 6-week progress reports quarterly," and "written comments and checklist for grades 6-8 in addition to report on pupil progress."

TABLE 23
PERCENTS OF SCHOOLS BY DIFFERENT GRADE
ORGANIZATIONS USING VARIOUS TYPES OF
STUDENT PROGRESS REPORTS

Types of Reports	Percent of Schools in Surveys		
	Elementary K/1-8	Middle Gr. 6-8	Jr. High Gr. 7-9
Letter Scale	91	85	89
Word Scale	31	21	11
Number Scale	12	13	9
Satisfactory/ unsatisfactory	55	39	27
Informal Written Notes	63	64	51
Percentage Marks	35	29	30
Dual System	8	9	10
Regular Parent Conferences	80	67	55
Self Evaluation	4	4	5

Teacher Advisory Plans

The use of teacher advisory plans in a homebase, homeroom, or advisor/advisee (A/A) organization has become more prevalent in the middle and junior high schools organizations than the elementary: 20 percent of the latter responded "yes," as compared with 39 percent of the other middle grade groupings, to the question: "Do you have a homebase or advisory (A/A) plan?" However, Table 24 shows that 68 percent of the elementary type said they used homebase teachers for counseling students as compared with 44 and 29 percent, respectively, for middle and junior high types. Part-time counselors were also used more frequently in the elementary type, with full-time counselors used in only 20 percent of these as compared with 84 and 92 percent, respectively, in the middle and junior high school types. With their reliance for counseling on persons other than full-time counselors, it is not surprising that 23 of the elementary schools wrote in "principal" as one of those counseling students, with the following also supplied one or more times: coach, nurse, vice-principal, psychologist, resource room teacher.

Almost identical percents of the schools with teacher advisory programs had daily ones, with similar small percents having them one to four times per week (see Table 25). The data (see Table 26) as to the length of period indicated quite

25

a spread in each type of school, with the majority of the elementary (54 percent) and the middle school types (63 percent) having more than 15 minutes per period, and the percent (47) of junior highs a little less.

TABLE 24
PERCENTS OF SCHOOLS BY DIFFERENT GRADE ORGANIZATIONS USING CERTAIN PERSONS FOR COUNSELING STUDENTS

Personnel	Percent of Schools in Surveys		
	Elementary K/1-8	Middle Gr. 6-8	Jr. High Gr. 7-9
Home Base Teacher	68	44	29
Other Classroom Teachers	35	31	26
Part-time Counselors	48	22	11
Full-time Counselors	20	84	92

TABLE 25
PERCENTS OF SCHOOLS BY DIFFERENT GRADE ORGANIZATIONS HAVING CERTAIN NUMBER OF ADVISORY PERIODS PER WEEK

Number of Periods Per Week	Percent of Schools in Surveys		
	Elementary K/1-8	Middle Gr. 6-8	Jr. High Gr. 7-9
1	11	10	7
2	5	8	10
3	5	4	5
4	0	1	0
5	79	78	78

TABLE 26
PERCENTS OF SCHOOLS BY DIFFERENT GRADE ORGANIZATIONS HAVING CERTAIN LENGTHS OF ADVISORY PERIODS

Minutes	Percent of Schools in Surveys		
	Elementary K/1-8	Middle Gr. 6-8	Jr. High Gr. 7-9
1 - 5	6	2	3
6 - 10	25	21	38
11 - 15	13	15	13
16 - 20	31	19	15
21 - 25	6	13	3
26 - 30	6	15	8
31 - 35	0	1	0
36 - 40	0	5	3
41 -45	6	4	10
46 -50	6	2	3
51 - 55	0	1	5
56 - 60	0	2	0
More than 60	0	1	0

Faculty with Special Preparation for Middle Grades Teaching

Table 27 reveals the disappointing but important lack of special preparation for large portions of middle grades faculties. The percent (32) of elementary schools with faculties of whom less than 25 percent have had special preparation is considerably less than that of the middle and junior high types. However, it should be noted that preparation in many states for elementary schools has traditionally included grades K-8 and that for secondary schools, grades 7-12. Thus the 28 percent of the elementary and 25 percent of the junior high school types responding that over three-fourths (76-100 percent) of their faculties had special preparation does not necessarily mean that this preparation focused on new middle school organization, program, and instruction.

The success of a special grade organization for the middle school years depends in large measure, the authors and indeed middle school educators in general believe, on increasing and improving special preparation programs for middle level teachers. The Carnegie Task Force report cited earlier recommended that: "Teachers in middle grade schools should be selected and specially educated to teach young adolescents." The report further stressed the importance of this recommendation in the following statement:

> This situation must change drastically. The success of the transformed middle grade school will stand or fall on the willingness of teachers and other staff to invest their efforts in the young adolescent students. Teachers must understand and want to teach young adolescents and find the middle grade school a rewarding place to work. (p.58)

TABLE 27
PERCENTS OF SCHOOLS BY DIFFERENT
GRADE ORGANIZATIONS HAVING FACULTIES
WITH VARIOUS EXTENTS OF SPECIAL
MIDDLE LEVEL PREPARATION

Percent of Faculty	Percent of Schools in Surveys		
	Elementary K/1-8	Middle Gr. 6-8	Jr. High Gr. 7-9
Less than 25%	32	61	46
25% to 50%	23	16	17
51% to 75%	17	15	12
76% to 100%	28	8	25

Inservice education can and does help, and its increase and improvement for teachers and principals in service is certainly desirable, but for middle level education to serve fully its unique role well-prepared and committed faculties and their leaders are essential.

Attitudes Toward the Middle Grades School Organization

The schools' responses to the question regarding the perceived attitudes of certain groups toward the middle grades organization showed a generally very favorable attitude toward the organization they had (see Table 28). For each group — students, staff, parents, and public — the percent of elementary schools respondents checking "Favorable" was slightly less, suggesting a slightly less satisfied group. But, all in all, the usual bias favoring one's own school that is characteristic of such surveys is here, too.

TABLE 28
PERCENTS OF SCHOOLS BY DIFFERENT GRADE
ORGANIZATIONS REPORTING CERTAIN
ATTITUDES OF SELECTED GROUPS
TOWARD THEIR MIDDLE SCHOOL

Attitudes	Percent of Schools in Surveys		
	Elementary K/1-8	Middle Gr. 6-8	Jr. High Gr. 7-9
Students Favorable	81	92	88
Indifferent	14	7	11
Opposed	5	0	1
Staff Favorable	88	94	90
Indifferent	7	5	7
Opposed	5	1	3
Parents Favorable	87	94	91
Indifferent	11	6	7
Opposed	3	0	2
Public Favorable	75	80	83
Indifferent	23	20	15
Opposed	2	0	2

Plans for Evaluation

The respondents listed many plans for evaluation of their schools and several enclosed copies of locally developed survey forms and reports they had used. Some indicated a need for additional plans and others that plans were in the development stage. The most frequent answers were those relating to the school's own plan of a survey, self-study, quality review, or other evaluation device involving staff and parents. "State standards" and "central office directed plan" were also frequently mentioned, and plans reported by one school included "administrative observation." The returns on this question were very similar in both surveys, and our comment on the plans reported in the 1987-88 one is applicable: "The generally more frequent, specific and comprehensive replies to the open-ended questions on evaluation in 1988 confirm the observation that evaluation of schools has become far more common and better done in the past 20 years" (Alexander & McEwin, 1989b, p. 44). We concluded after our elementary school supplemental survey that evaluations seem equally important and similarly conducted in the several types of middle grade organizations.

Problems of Including Middle Grades in Elementary Schools

Respondents were also asked to list "major problems you have encountered, if any, in having the middle grades included in your school." The most frequently mentioned problem was "discipline of students in upper grades," with "scheduling of enrichment programs," a close second. Related to the latter also are "limited electives" and "too few students." Also mentioned by more than one school were "safety of younger pupils," "communication problems," "lack of trained teachers," "inflexibility," and "poor facility." Other interesting problems reported by individual schools only were "lack of parental involvement," "different philosophy" (of lower and upper grades), "divergent goals," "split classes," "alcohol and drugs."

Several of these problems are related to the advantages and disadvantages of having middle grades in elementary schools reported next, and to the overall issue summarized in Section III.

Advantages and Disadvantages of Elementary Type

A concluding question in our survey asked: "What are some advantages and disadvantages in having the middle grades (5-8) and the lower elementary grades housed in the same school?" The most frequently mentioned advantages were "buddy system" and "peer tutoring." The major advantage here may be for the lower grades although there are certainly values for the older students who are the "buddies" and "tutors," too. "Flexibility," "ease of communication," "continuity," "sense of belonging" (that is, presumably, for more years in one school), and "better chance that progress can be followed" (longer), were each also mentioned by individual respondents.

Regarding disadvantages, some responses mentioned were the opposites of the advantages cited: "older students set bad examples for younger students," and "attitude of superiority" (of older students). Other disadvantages cited frequently were "discipline problems," "limited extra-curricular," "scheduling," and "sharing play equipment." Our summary of the pros and cons of having the middle grades in elementary schools is presented in the next section.

III

Should the Middle Grades Be In Elementary Schools?

The authors cannot give a "yes" or "no" answer to this question on the basis of our surveys—we can and will give, however, a summary of the strengths and weaknesses indicated by the surveys of present elementary type middle grades arrangements and a few suggestions for their strengthening. This summary is based on examination of our data with references to the criteria of good schools in the middle cited in Section I. As explained there, these are the same criteria that were used in our earlier reports on separate schools in the middle, and they are encompassed, we believe, in the report of the Carnegie Task Force on Education of Young Adolescents referenced earlier. It is relevant, too, to note that these same criteria were used in the ASCD survey (Cawelti, 1988) of middle level schools as to their status in 1988, with findings very similar to those on this phase of our own survey conducted the same year. These criteria and our discussions of the relevant data from our studies regarding each follow.

1. An interdisciplinary organization with a flexibly scheduled day. Despite the relative smallness of many of the middle grades enrollment in the elementary schools, and the opportunity therefore available for informal and flexible arrangements for teaming, the percent of elementary type schools practicing departmentalization in grade 6 is almost as large as in the middle school type. The self-contained classroom plan is more common in grades 6, 7 and 8 of the elementary schools than in the middle schools, although even in the former no more common than departmentalization in grade 6 and much less (about 1 to 3) in grades 7 and 8. Interdisciplinary team plans are found in only 10 to 14 percent of basic subjects in the elementary schools' grades 6, 7, and 8, compared with 24 to 41 percent of these grades in middle schools.

An examination of scheduling practices revealed that the self-contained classroom schedule with its great possibilities of flexibility and subject integration is no longer dominant in the middle grades of the K-8 elementary school. The uniform daily period characteristic of secondary schools prevailed in over half (53 percent) of the elementary type schools in grade 6, and in over two-thirds of their grades 7 and 8. Flexible scheduling was reported by less than 10 percent for either grade 6, 7, or 8 of the elementary type, as compared with 30, 25, and 21 percent of these grades in middle schools.

We are forced to conclude that the middle grades in elementary schools are not using their relative smallness and traditional closeness and informality to advantage with reference to Criterion 1. Schools of this type would do well to train or employ personnel qualified and interested in interdisciplinary instruction with flexible scheduling and provide them facilities and teaching schedules to make possible the many advantages of this plan of organization.

The Carnegie Task Force report, *Turning Points,* made this strong argument for the interdisciplinary plan:

> A better approach [than departmentalization] is to create teams of teachers and students who work together to achieve academic and personal goals for students. Teachers share responsibility for the same students and can solve problems together, often before they reach the crisis stage; teachers report that classroom problems are dramatically reduced through teaming. This community of learning nurtures bonds between teacher and student that are the building blocks of the education of the young adolescent. (p. 38)

2. An adequate guidance program including a teacher advisory plan. Only 20 percent of the elementary type schools had a homebase or advisory plan as compared with 39 percent of the other middle grade groupings. But as we noted earlier, 68 percent of the K-8 elementary schools used homebase teachers for counseling students as compared with 44 and 29 percent, respectively, of middle and junior high types. Of course the latter's increased size helped them to have far more full-time counselors. We believe it is positive that many elementary schools reported use of the principal as a counselor. Most schools of all types had daily advisory periods with considerable variation as to their length, more of the elementary than the junior high but fewer than the middle school having more than 15 minutes per period.

Regardless of the advisory plan followed, we consider it essential that teachers serve as advisors, along with other school personnel as trained and available. It should be relatively easy, organizationally speaking, to organize, staff, and schedule a homebase program utilizing all team teachers and others as available and qualified with each teacher having in his or her homebase a relatively small number of students. This program should be more easily arranged and more effective in interdisciplinary and possibly self-contained organizations. These recommendations from The Carnegie Task Force report are relevant.

> Teachers in a restructured middle school will need education in principles of guidance to serve as advisors. Teachers will also need preparation in working with one and two parent families, families of various ethnic and racial backgrounds and families who for economic or other reasons are undergoing stress that may influence their children's performance in school. (p. 59)

3. A full scale exploratory program. The exploratory program of the junior high school, perhaps its distinguishing and most significant contribution, has been continued in the middle schools and is found, but to a lesser extent, in the middle grades of the elementary school type. Thus, Tables 6, 7, and 8 show the comparable provision in grades 6-8 of these two organizations, for required Art, Music, and Reading, with considerable smaller percents of the other traditional exploratories: Foreign Language, Home Economics, and Industrial Arts.

Certain newer exploratory subjects (See Tables 9, 10, and 11) — Careers, Computers, Creative Writing, Health and Sex Education — are required in grades 6, 7, and 8 even more frequently in the elementary than in the middle school type, with similar, smaller percents of these and the other subjects listed on an elective basis. As to other curriculum opportunities, mostly "activities," the elementary type offers most of these just as widely as the middle and junior high types. Interschool sports for both boys and girls are offered more frequently in grade 6 in the elementary type while intramurals are offered less frequently in the elementary school than in the middle and junior high. Nearly all of the other opportunities — Arts and Crafts, Honor Society, Photography, School Parties, Social Dances, and Student Council — are offered by somewhat smaller percents of the elementary than the other types.

Thus middle graders attending an elementary school are not likely to miss most opportunities for the exploration and initial development of worthwhile interests, although they might be slightly less likely to have the last listed ones.

4. Curriculum provision for such broad goals and curriculum domains as personal development, continued learning skills, and basic knowledge areas. Table 15 shows that 100 percent of the elementary type schools in the middle provide the four basic subjects all year for each grade, with slightly smaller percents of the middle and junior highs except in math, and with 97 percent of the elementary schools providing physical education so fully as compared with 80 and 70 percent of the middle and junior high schools, respectively. The personal development domain is provided for through the exploratory, the guidance, and the health and physical education programs, and in only the guidance and some exploratory areas have we noted smaller percents of the elementary type meeting this criterion. As to skills of continued learning, both reading and computers were shown in earlier tables to be required more frequently in grades 6, 7, and 8 of elementary than middle and junior high type schools.

So we again must recognize that middle grade students in elementary schools are almost as likely, even more likely in a few aspects, to have as comprehensive a curriculum as those in middle and junior high schools.

5. Varied and effective instructional methodology for the age group. It was impossible, we believed, to secure adequate data through our surveys for making judgments as to the extent schools in the survey met this criterion. We were very much interested in the comparable availability of the independent study opportunities considered essential for the middle graders' growth in learning skills and interests. The 1968 and 1988 data had shown considerable increase in

33

the provisions of independent study opportunities in the latter year in middle and junior high school types. No data were secured for the elementary type in 1968, but the survey data shown in Table 22 indicated the considerable greater availability of release from class part or all of the time for independent study in 1988 of grades 6, 7, and 8 students in the elementary type schools (60 percent or more) as compared with about 25 to 30 percent of the schools in the other types. About twice the percent of the elementary as compared with the others provide individually planned programs with regularly scheduled independent study times.

The data we secured on grouping for instruction and on student progress reports (Table 23) are also relevant to instructional methodology. As to grouping we noted earlier that the elementary type schools seemed most willing to use the least selective criteria for grouping. And as to student progress reports, the elementary type used non-letter scale marks and regular parent/teacher conferences more frequently than others. Thus, evidence indicates that more concern for individual students is indicated in smaller elementary schools than through the features of independent study, grouping, and progress reports noted.

6. Continued orientation and articulation for students, parents, and teachers. As noted earlier, Table 4 showed relatively small differences between the percents of the three types using the means of articulation included. Smaller percents of elementary schools used these means: "joint workshops with teacher in lower and higher grades;" "joint curriculum planning with teachers of higher and/or lower grades;" and "middle school students taking courses in high schools." A question focusing on orientation activities was not included in the elementary survey since the middle grades in these schools have usually been there a long time. It is when the middle grades are moved into a new school that the needs for orientation and preparatory activities become very important.

Closing Comments.
Our surveys do not yield an unequivocal answer to the question of whether the middle grades belong in the elementary organization or elsewhere, especially in a separate middle level school. A somewhat similar conclusion was reached for the sixth grade only in Lounsbury and Johnston's (1988) report of a national shadow study of grade 6 in 1987: "The shadow study data do not show that sixth grades in elementary schools are providing better programs than sixth grades in middle schools — or worse programs." (p. 108). We concur in their further judgment as expressed so well in the following paragraph we believe to be equally applicable to grades 7 and 8:

> Each type of school has advantages and disadvantages. The answer to the question, "Where does the sixth grade belong?" is not to be found in the administrative unit that houses it. Many other factors must be considered — the nature of the school program above and below, school size, the competence and attitudes of faculty, for instance. The key question to ask is, "Where can sixth graders' educational and developmental needs best be met given the conditions prevailing in the local situation?" (p. 110)

Epstein and Mac Iver (1990) came to much the same conclusion based on their national study of 1,753 schools of various grade organizations containing grade seven. "With the information available at this time, neither we nor any one can say for sure that there is one "best" grade span or program for all middle grades in the U.S. (p. 92).

Our data do indicate that more schools in one of these organizations are more likely to meet each of certain criteria than the other. Thus the comparisons of percents indicated that: (1) the elementary type schools had slightly higher percents of the four basic subjects and physical education required for all students: (2) instruction in basic skills or reading and computer usage; (3) independent study opportunities; and (4) the more individualized and flexible types of grouping and student progress reports.

The percents of middle schools were larger for: (1) interdisciplinary teaming, (2) flexible scheduling, (3) use of teacher advisory programs, (4) articulation efforts, (5) more comprehensive traditional exploratory courses and current activities; and (6) more intramural programs at all levels and fewer interschool sports at the sixth grade level. It is significant to note that many of the components found more frequently in middle schools are those most often identified in the literature as developmentally appropriate for middle level youth.

Our own judgment is that in communities where a consolidated middle school is not feasible and where the middle grade enrollments are small, those communities would probably be as well or better off helping their grades 6-8 in elementary schools become strong units that focussed on early adolescents. In many such cases, retraining of faculties is definitely needed to develop fully a middle school unit meeting such criteria as we have used. But smallness, informality, and closeness are strong arguments, we think, against moving to a separate middle school that is too small and poor to have the facilities and numbers required for a fully diversified, adequate middle school program. As we have seen, however, smallness in the elementary type has not always been accompanied by such desirable practices as the interdisciplinary teaming (some schools have too few teachers) and teacher advisory programs the Carnegie Task Force associated with relatively small numbers to create the needed "communities for learning" in schools in the middle.

Nevertheless, if the middle grades are cramped, the school population expanding, and the program relatively unlike that of a good middle school, the faster the move can be made to a middle school facility, well planned, staffed, and programmed, the better. And our data, as presented especially in our 1988 survey report, would argue for this new school to be a grades 6-8 (or 5-8 if necessary) one, with no grade 9 or other junior high school label. The junior high school may be best, of course, if the move necessitated is that of grades 7-8 from the elementary and grade 9 from the high school, and if all three units — elementary, junior and senior high — share in the planning of the new organizations with the full faculty and program preparation needed.

Most of all, we would argue for the type of school for students in the middle grades that can be staffed most certainly by teachers competent in their craft, interested in working with this age group and committed to making the adjustments in ways of working, schedules, and teaching assignments necessary. As Lounsbury and Johnston (1988) asserted:

> The teacher makes the difference. It is not school unit, grade organization, interdisciplinary teaming, relevant curriculum content, or anything else, that is the essential factor in the improvement of middle level education. It is the quality of the classroom teacher. (p. 112)

To secure and hold such teachers requires much planning and hard work of school districts, teacher preparation institutions, and professional organizations. We cannot be satisfied with the present situation where most middle level school faculty members have no special preparation for their roles in the new units. The middle grades represent a third level, the middle level between the elementary and secondary levels of education. This intermediate level must be known and enhanced, with appropriate preparatory training, certification, employment, and compensation of faculties comparable to the other levels. As this goal is reached, there should be decreasing debate as to which grade organization is best for the middle grades. The problem may become: "How can we provide the faculty members and leaders essential to having an excellent program for our young adolescent students in the middle grades?"

References

Alexander, W. M. & McEwin, C. K. (1989a). *Earmarks of schools in the middle: A research report.* Boone, North Carolina: Appalachian State University.

Alexander, W. M. & McEwin, C. K. (1989b). *Schools in the middle: Status and progress.* Columbus, Ohio: National Middle School Association.

Carnegie Council on Adolescent Development (1989). *Turning points: Preparing American youth for the 21st century.* Washington, DC: Carnegie Corporation.

Cawelti, G. (November, 1988). Middle schools a better match with early adolescents needs, ASCD survey finds. *ASCD Curriculum Update.*

Epstein, J. L. & Mac Iver, D. J. (1990). The middle grades: Is grade span the important issue? *Educational Horizons, 68*(2), 88-94.

Lounsbury, J. H. & Johnston, J. H. (1988). *Life in the three 6th grades.* Reston, Virginia: National Association of Secondary School Principals.

National Center for Educational Statistics (1989). *Digest of educational statistics.* Washington, DC: U. S. Government Printing Office.

Appendix

APPALACHIAN STATE UNIVERSITY
DEPARTMENT OF CURRICULUM AND INSTRUCTION
BOONE, NC 28608

MIDDLE GRADES EDUCATION
IN THE ELEMENTARY SCHOOL SURVEY, 1988

Your school has been selected in a nationwide sample of K/1-8 schools. Your cooperation in completing and returning this form promptly will be greatly appreciated, and you will be sent a copy of the survey report if requested below.

This survey is Part II of a national study of programs and practices in the middle grades. The overall purpose is to find out more about the status and progress of middle level education. Research in middle grades education has too long been restricted primarily to programs housed separately from the elementary and senior high school. This survey focuses on middle grades (4th-8th) in schools also containing lower elementary grades. Survey results should help focus increased attention to the important role of middle grades programs whether or not they are a part of a separate middle level school.

C. Kenneth McEwin
Professor
Appalachian State University
Boone, NC 28608

ŎŎŎ

GENERAL INFORMATION

1. Name_____Title_____
2. Name of School_____Current Enrollment_____
3. School Address_____City_____State_____Zip___
4. School District___No. Elementary Schools in District___
5. Do you wish to be sent a copy of the report of this
   survey? Yes_____ No____

ADMINISTRATIVE ORGANIZATION

1.Please indicate by a check the grades included in your school, 1987-88:
   − K-8   − 1-8   − Other
2.Please indicate by as many checks as applicable the housing arrangements for students:
One plant (all grades)
− "Schools within a school" plan, each school a separate area
− Certain grades in separate buildings on the same campus
− Some students housed in building(s) on another campus
− Housed in a plant with lower and/or higher grades
− Other (specify)_____

38

3.Please indicate by a check any of the following means employed by your school
to provide articulation between your school and those with higher grades:
  − Joint workshops with teachers in higher grades
  − Joint curriculum planning activities with teachers of higher grades
  − Teacher visitation of high schools
  − Sharing faculty with high schools
  − Giving program information to high schools
  − Providing data re students leaving your school
  − Student visitation of the high school(s) for orientation
  − Visitation of your school by high school orientation representatives
  − Middle grades students taking advanced course work in the high school
  − Other (specify)_____

ESTABLISHMENT OF YOUR SCHOOL
4.Please indicate by a check the year your school was established:
  − Before 1955 − 1955-62 − 1963-71 − 1972-79 − 1980-87

Common Subjects   CURRICULUM
5.Please indicate by checks as applicable whether each of these subjects is taken
by all students in grades 4-8 (all year) and explain the situation for each "No":

Subject	Check		Explanation if "No"
	Yes	No	
Language Arts	I		
Mathematics	I		
Physical Education	I		
Science	I		
Social Studies	I		

Required Exploratories, Electives, Etc.
6.Please place a check in each box to indicate a required course at each grade level.
Also, please indicate the length of time each course is offered:

Course	In What Grades					Length of Course		
	4	5	6	7	8	Year	1/2 Year	Less than 1/2 Year
Agriculture								
Art								
Band								
Careers								
Chorus								
Computers								
Creative Writing								
Foreign Lang.								
General Music								
Health								
Home Ec.								
Industrial Arts								
Journalism								
Orchestra								
Reading								
Sex Education								
Speech								
Typing								
Others:*								

*If your list includes too many others to list here, please just enclose a copy
with information noted as to grades as above.

Exploratories, Electives, Etc.

7. Please place a check in each box to indicate an elective course that is <u>available</u>
<u>but not required</u> at each grade level. Also, please indicate the length of time each
course is offered:

Course	In What Grades					Length of Course		
	4	5	6	7	8	Year	1/2 Year	Less than 1/2 Year
Agriculture								
Art								
Band								
Careers								
Chorus								
Computers								
Creative Writing								
Foreign Lang.								
General Music								
Health								
Home Ec.								
Industrial Arts								
Journalism								
Orchestra								
Reading								
Sex Education								
Speech								
Typing								
Others:*								

*If your list includes too many others to list here, please just enclose a copy
with information noted as to grades as above.

Other Curriculum Opportunities (Elective Activities, Minicourses, etc.)

8. Please indicate by as many checks as applicable in what grades each of the
following is offered, if at all, and add any special notes:

Activity	If Offered In What Grades					Notes
	4	5	6	7	8	
Arts and Crafts						
Honor Society						
Intramural Sports (Boys)						
Intramural Sports (Girls)						
Interschool Sports (Boys)						
Interschool Sports (Girls)						
Photography						
Publications						
School Parties						
Social Dancing						
Student Council						
Others:*						

*If your list includes too many others to list here, please just enclose a copy
with information noted as to grades as above.

INSTRUCTION

Instructional Organization

9.Please write in the grade(s) in which each instructional plan is followed for the subjects listed:

	In what grade(s) (write in) is the plan followed for each subject				
Instructional Plan	Lang Arts	Math	Science	Soc. St.	Others(write in subject & grade
Interdisciplinary Team —(2 or more teachers working together with same students in 2 or more of these subjects)					
Departmental — (different class and teacher each subject)					
Self-contained classroom—(one teacher for all the basic subjects)					
Other plan— Explain: _____					

Special Notes:

Grouping for Instruction

10.Please indicate by as many checks as applicable the criteria employed in assigning students to various types of classroom groups at each grade level:

Criteria	Type of Grouping		
	Homebase (advisory group)	Instructional groups for basic subjects	Instructional groups in elective offerings
	4 I 5 I 6 I 7 I 8	4 I 5 I 6 I 7 I 8	4 I 5 I 6 I 7 I 8
I.Q. Tests			
Achievement Tests			
Teacher Recommendations			
Age (i.e., # years in school)			
Previous Academic Record			
Random Assignment			

Instructional Schedule

11. Please indicate by as many checks as applicable the type(s) of daily scheduling utilized in your school at each grade level

Type of Schedule	4	5	6	7	8
Self-contained classrooms					
Daily periods uniform in length					
Flexible scheduling within blocks for teams					
Daily periods of varying length					
Other plan (describe):					

Independent Study

12. Please indicate by grades, any subject(s) in which opportunities are provided for some students to work independently of a class:

	Write in, by grades, any subject (s) in which used				
Type of Independent Study	4	5	6	7	8

Reporting Pupil Progress

13. Please indicate by as many checks as applicable the system(s) your school uses for reporting pupil progress to parents:
    - Letter scale (A to F, etc.)
    - Word scale (Excellent, good, etc.)
    - Number scale (1-5, etc.)
    - Satisfactory-Unsatisfactory scale (S,U; E, S, U; Pass-Fail, Etc.)
    - Informal written notes
    - Percentage marks (92, 80, etc.)
    - Dual system (progress compared (1) with the class and (2) with student's own potential)
    - Regularly-scheduled parent conferences
    - Self-evaluation
    - Other (specify)

Is there a distinction between the system of reporting pupil progress in academic and exploratory elective courses?
- Yes - No If yes, please explain: _____

14. Please indicate by as many checks as applicable the persons in your school who are assigned the responsibility for counseling students:
    - Home base teacher (advisor)   - Full-time counselors

    - Other classroom teachers   - Other (specify)

    - Part-time counselors   _____

15. Do you have a home base or advisory (A/A) plan?___Yes ___No. If yes, please supply this information:

(1) Do all teachers serve as home base teachers or advisors?

Notes re exceptions:

Yes ___ _____

No ___ _____

(2) Which, if any, staff members other than teachers also serve as advisors?

_____

(3) How many times per week do the home base or advisory groups meet?

Daily _____ If not, how many times per week? _____

(4) How many minutes per session does the home base or advisory group meet?

16. Please check the approximate percent of your faculty who have had specific university or college preparation for middle level teaching:

less than 25% – 25 to 50% – 51 to 75% – 76 to 100%

SCHOOL EVALUATION

17. Please indicate by as many checks as applicable your estimate of the attitude of each of the following groups toward your grade level school organization:

Group	Estimate of Group's Attitude			Notes
	Favorable	Indifferent	Opposed	
Students				
Staff				
Parents				
Public				

Please describe any plan you have for evaluating your school, enclosing any available illustrative materials:

Please list any major problems you have encountered, if any, in having the middle grades (4-8) included in your school:

What are some major advantages and/or disadvantages in having the middle grades (4-8) and the lower elementary grades housed in the same school?

Advantages:

Disadvantages:

Other Comments:

43

PUBLICATIONS
National Middle School Association

A Middle School Curriculum: From Rhetoric to Reality
James A. Beane (83 pages).. $8.00

Visions of Teaching and Learning: Eighty Exemplary
Middle Level Projects John Arnold (160 pages)...................$12.00

The New American Family and the School
J. Howard Johnston (48 pages) $6.00

Who They Are - How We Teach: Early Adolescents
and Their Teachers
C. Kenneth McEwin and Julia T. Thomason (32 pages) $4.00

The Japanese Junior High School: A View From The
Inside Paul S. George (56 pages)... $5.00

Schools in the Middle: Status and Progress
William M. Alexander and C. Kenneth McEwin (112 pages)........$10.00

A Journey Through Time: A Chronology of Middle Level
Resources Edward J. Lawton (36 pages)................................. $5.00

Dynamite in the Classroom: A How-To Handbook for
Teachers Sandra L. Schurr (272 pages)................................$15.00

Developing Effective Middle Schools Through Faculty
Participation. Second and Enlarged Edition
Elliot Y. Merenbloom (108 pages).. $8.50

Preparing to Teach in Middle Level Schools
William M. Alexander and C. Kenneth McEwin (76 pages)........... $7.00

Guidance in the Middle Level Schools: Everyone's
Responsibility Claire Cole (34 pages) $5.00

Young Adolescent Development and School Practices:
Promoting Harmony John Van Hoose & David Strahan
(68 pages).. $7.00

When the Kids Come First: Enhancing Self-Esteem
James A. Beane and Richard P. Lipka (96 pages)....................... $8.00

Interdisciplinary Teaching: Why and How
Gordon F. Vars (56 pages).. $6.00

Cognitive Matched Instruction in Action
Esther Fusco and Associates (36 pages)...................................... $5.00

The Middle School Donald H. Eichhorn (128 pages)................... $6.00

Long-Term Teacher-Student Relationships: A Middle
School Case Study Paul George (30 pages)......................... $4.00

Positive Discipline: A Pocketful of Ideas
William Purkey and David Strahan (56 pages) $6.00

Teachers as Inquirers: Strategies for Learning With and
About Early Adolescents Chris Stevenson (52 pages).......... $6.00

Adviser-Advisee Programs: Why, What, and How
Michael James (75 pages)... $7.00

What Research Says to the Middle Level Practitioner
J. Howard Johnston and Glenn C. Markle (112 pages)................... $8.00

Evidence for the Middle School
Paul George and Lynn Oldaker (52 pages)................................. $6.00

Involving Parents in Middle Level Education
John W. Myers (52 pages)... $6.00

Perspectives: Middle Level Education
John H. Lounsbury, Editor (190 pages).....................................$10.00

The Team Process: A Handbook for Teachers, Second and
Enlarged Edition Elliot Y. Merenbloom (120 pages).............. $8.00

This We Believe NMSA Committee (24 pages)........................ $3.50

Teacher to Teacher Nancy Doda (64 pages)............................ $6.00

Early Adolescence: A Time of Change-Implications
for Schools Videocassette (37 minutes) $75.00

Early Adolescence: A Time of Change-Implications
for Parents Videocassette and Utilization Guide (50 minutes)....$80.00

NMSA, 4807 Evanswood Drive, Columbus, Ohio 43229-6292
(614) 848-8211   FAX (614) 848-4301